LAS VEGAS

THE CITY AT A GLANCE

CW00502416

Rio All-Suite
It might host the World Series o
surer bets at the Rio are its carni
a flying stage and the view from
3700 W Flamingo Road, T 777 7777

Luxor
Encased in 4.5 hectares of glass, the Veldon
Simpson-designed Luxor resort is modelled
on the pyramids and features a giant sphinx.
See p074

Mandarin Oriental
CityCenter's sophisticated non-gaming hotel
is topped by Pierre Gagnaire's appropriately
high-end restaurant Twist (see p037).
3752 Las Vegas Boulevard South, T 590 8888

Trump International
Like a 190m gold bar jutting into the skyline,
this 2008 condo-hotel is pure Donald Trump.
2000 Fashion Show Drive, T 982 0000

World Market Center
This geometric behemoth of a furniture
showroom, which was designed by The Jerde
Partnership, opened its doors in 2005. It's
the *only* place to deck out your casino resort.
495 S Grand Central Parkway, T 599 9621

Stratosphere Tower
At 350m, the tallest structure in Vegas
majors on hair-raising thrill rides and an
observation deck unrivalled in the city.
See p012

Downtown
Old Vegas, with its gangster-era casinos, is
being rediscovered. Moving in are galleries
and upscale bars with downscale prices, while
Symphony Park became the site of a centre
for performing arts in 2012 (see p068).

INTRODUCTION
THE CHANGING FACE OF THE URBAN SCENE

Twenty-four hours in Las Vegas is something everyone should try once. A shock of neon in the desert, it's a surreal place with a gaudy, fluorescent plumage and a glamorised past, when showgirls were dames and guys were mobsters, and tourists flocked to marvel at the mushroom clouds from the nuclear testing in the desert.

Now, in the midst of an economic downturn, investors who bet on the black have ended up in the red, filing for bankruptcy before even cashing the first chip. Yet, while markets struggle worldwide, you wouldn't know it by Las Vegas' 40 million visitors a year. This city has the ability to reinvent itself and keep luxury and spectacle at the forefront. Starchitects have replaced a tradition of pastiche with one of panache; celebrity chefs have transformed the cuisine; and Downtown has begun its reinvention, as a nascent arts scene takes hold and young bar owners create a contemporary cocktail culture. The mega hotels are creating mini offshoots, boutique only by Vegas standards, but it is a move in the right direction. And the one constant is the remarkable desert scenery.

Of course, the motto 'What happens in Vegas stays in Vegas' invites excess. This is the most un-PC of cities. Boobs are big. Plastic is fantastic. Ladies get in free. It can feel like a *Carry On* set, notably when the centurions appear at Caesars. And, yes, you have to look past the washed-up characters on the slots, but now there is so much more to see, plenty of it surprising and all of it interesting.

ESSENTIAL INFO
FACTS, FIGURES AND USEFUL ADDRESSES

TOURIST OFFICE
3150 Paradise Road
T 892 0711
www.visitlasvegas.com

TRANSPORT
Airport transfer to city centre
ASC and Bell Trans run a shuttle service
($7 to the Strip; $8.50 to Downtown)
Car hire
Hertz
T 1 800 654 3131
www.hertz.com
Helicopter
Papillon
T 736 7243
www.papillon.com
Monorail
T 699 8299
www.lvmonorail.com
Trains run from 7am to 12am on Mondays;
7am to 2am, Tuesday to Thursday; 7am to
3am, Friday to Sunday. One-day pass, $12
Taxis
Desert Cab
T 386 9102
There are taxi ranks outside most resorts

EMERGENCY SERVICES
Emergencies
T 911
24-hour pharmacy
CVS
2425 E Desert Inn Road
T 734 0258

CONSULATE
British Consulate-General
Suite 1350, 2029 Century Park East
Los Angeles
T 310 481 0031
www.gov.uk/government/world/usa

POSTAL SERVICES
Post office
201 Las Vegas Boulevard South
T 1 800 275 8777
Shipping
UPS
2550 E Desert Inn Road
T 369 5920

BOOKS
Beneath the Neon by Matthew O'Brien
(Huntington Press)
Learning from Las Vegas
by Robert Venturi, Denise Scott Brown
and Steven Izenour (MIT Press)
Neon Boneyard: Las Vegas A-Z by
Judy Natal (University of Chicago Press)

WEBSITES
Architecture
www.aialasvegas.org
Newspaper
www.lvrj.com

EVENTS
Neon Reverb
www.neonreverb.com
World Series of Poker
www.wsop.com

COST OF LIVING
Taxi from McCarran International
Airport to Downtown
$20
Cappuccino
$3
Packet of cigarettes
$5
Daily newspaper
$0.50
Bottle of champagne
$150

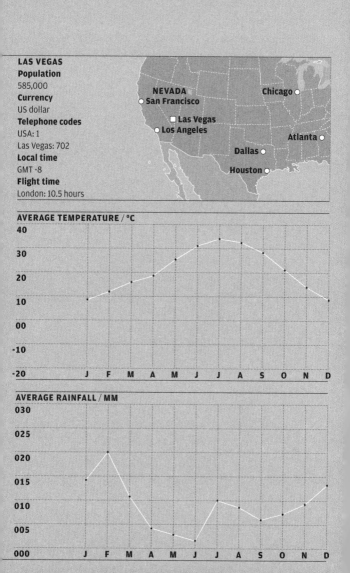

LAS VEGAS
Population
585,000
Currency
US dollar
Telephone codes
USA: 1
Las Vegas: 702
Local time
GMT -8
Flight time
London: 10.5 hours

NEVADA
San Francisco
Chicago
Las Vegas
Los Angeles
Atlanta
Dallas
Houston

AVERAGE TEMPERATURE / °C

J	F	M	A	M	J	J	A	S	O	N	D

40
30
20
10
00
-10
-20

AVERAGE RAINFALL / MM

030
025
020
015
010
005
000

J	F	M	A	M	J	J	A	S	O	N	D

NEIGHBOURHOODS
THE AREAS YOU NEED TO KNOW AND WHY

To help you navigate the city, we've chosen the most interesting districts (see below and the map inside the back cover) and colour-coded our featured venues, according to their location; those venues that are outside these areas are not coloured.

SOUTH STRIP

This stretch of the Vegas skyline includes a Statue of Liberty, an Egyptian pyramid and an Arthurian castle. The stylish Aria (see p024), Mandarin Oriental (see p016) and MGM's Skylofts (see p030) are among the top hotels here. This end of the Strip also makes for a swift transfer to McCarran Airport (the runway is round the corner) and a fast escape by road should you suddenly need to get the hell outta town.

NORTH STRIP

The Wynn (see p031) is the big draw here; north of the Convention Center there are few attractions apart from the Stratosphere Tower (see p012) and numerous wedding chapels. Redevelopment included the arrival of Donald Trump's condo-hotel tower, its facade lined with 24-carat gold, but other projects failed to take off. Without the foot traffic of the South Strip, the area appears doomed, and is often bypassed by taxis heading further north to Downtown.

DOWNTOWN

Although the Strip usurped Downtown as the heart of the Las Vegas action, this is where it all began, and regeneration is taking hold at last. Now, a visit to Fremont Street light show (see p014) can coincide with a bar crawl (see p040) and culture at Emergency Arts (see p070). West of Main Street, the Symphony Park development includes The Smith Center (see p068), a theatre and classical music venue.

CENTRE STRIP

Find the Strip's greatest concentration of good restaurants and nightclubs here. If you want a little class, hit the Bellagio (see p022) or the cool Cosmopolitan (see p017). For artifice, tour Venice, Rome and Paris, or catch the *Sirens of TI* show outside Treasure Island (3300 Las Vegas Boulevard South, T 894 7111) and the erupting volcano at The Mirage (3400 Las Vegas Boulevard South, T 791 7111).

ARTS DISTRICT

This little pocket of Downtown is gradually being colonised by small art galleries and is definitely on the up. It still tends towards the gritty rather than the refined, but boosted by the successful First Fridays, when the area's galleries and stores party all evening, the neighbourhood is turning into a bona fide arts and design zone, against the odds. Take a load off at the hip Artifice (see p038) and Bar + Bistro (T 202 6060) in The Arts Factory (see p080).

PARADISE

Officially, the Strip is in Paradise (where else?), but for the purposes of this guide, we've set the two apart. Much of Paradise reveals how, a few blocks from the Strip, Vegas is quite humdrum — all low-rise urban normality. However, the Hard Rock (see p023), sports hub Thomas & Mack Center (see p088) and the National Atomic Testing Museum (755 E Flamingo Road, T 794 5151) are well worth a visit.

LANDMARKS

THE SHAPE OF THE CITY SKYLINE

There is no getting around the fact that Las Vegas is the Strip. The city is growing apace and attracts 5,000 new residents a month, but the Strip remains its raison d'être – a 6.5km stretch of dreams and decadence officially named Las Vegas Boulevard South. It's not a boulevard in the promenadable sense. There are eight lanes of traffic and no pavement cafés, just one hulking resort after another. Hop around by cab, which you can pick up at any casino entrance (avoid early-evening gridlock), or drive (car parks are free). Some of the central resorts are linked by travelators, sky bridges or a tram; there's also a monorail that runs from the MGM Grand (see p030) to the Sahara, although the resort itself closed in 2011. Save strolling outdoors for the evening, when cooler temperatures and the sea of lights make it appealing. Should you go off-Strip, take a cab number with you, or you may struggle to get back again.

As for navigation, every building along the Strip is a landmark, from the cigarette lighter-esque Mandalay Bay (3950 Las Vegas Boulevard South, T 632 7777), past the bronzed Wynn (see p031) to the Stratosphere (see p012) en route to Downtown. Completing the compass are the Palms towers (see p020), on West Flamingo, and the Hard Rock (see p023) to the east. Everything can be spotted by just looking up – the only place you'll need satnav is inside the resorts, where all roads lead to the casino and not the exit.
For full addresses, see Resources.

Veer Towers

These twin condo towers, designed by Chicago firm Murphy/Jahn, bookmark the mammoth 2010 CityCenter complex that brought architects of the calibre of Rafael Viñoly, Kohn Pedersen Fox and Daniel Libeskind to Vegas. Each of the 37 storeys is offset by 24cm so that the towers 'veer' away from each other at five-degree angles (beating Pisa by about a degree). Plonking two glass boxes in the desert might have been deemed a punt too far, but Veer has fine eco credentials thanks to its aluminium louvres and chequerboard facades that feature yellow fritted glass. Lobbies house Brit Richard Long's giant mud artworks, dredged, oddly, from the River Avon. See if you can elicit an invite from a resident to the infinity pool and bar on the roof. *3780 Las Vegas Boulevard South, www.citycenter.com/veer*

Eiffel Tower, Paris Las Vegas

'Oh, it's beautiful. Just like the real thing,' we overheard a US guest saying at Paris Las Vegas. 'Not that I've been there.' The joy of Vegas for many Americans, post-9/11, is that they don't have to risk a flight to Paris, Venice, Luxor, or even New York. Because it's all here, in safe miniature or, in the case of the Campanile Tower at The Venetian (see p064), at 97 per cent of the actual size. It's easy to scoff, but much more fun to give yourself over to the architainment. Designed by Bergman, Walls & Associates, Paris Las Vegas opened in 1999 and the complex includes an Arc de Triomphe as well as the half-scale Eiffel Tower. You can take the elevator 140m up to the top deck, although the Stratosphere Tower (overleaf) offers better views.
*3655 Las Vegas Boulevard South,
T 727 4758, www.parislasvegas.com*

Stratosphere Tower

Go for the view, or to take your vows in the clouds. Effectively a sign for a 2,427-room hotel and casino, at 350m this structure is the tallest free-standing observation tower in the US. It is home to a revolving restaurant, wedding chapel and thrill rides, such as Insanity, which spins tourists 19.5m over the edge of the building, 113 storeys up – it's one way to see Downtown. The Stratosphere already evokes a less sensible age: its founder Bob Stupak, a World Series poker player, used to drive around town in a rocket car and nearly died in a motorbike crash in 1995. No one bet on him waking up from the coma but, true to form, he recovered for the launch of the Stratosphere in 1996 – only to see it go bust a year later and then be sold.
2000 Las Vegas Boulevard South,
T 380 7777, www.stratospherehotel.com

Fremont Street Experience

Should the 42in flatscreen TV in your suite not cut it, head to Fremont Street to see the 'biggest screen on the planet'. It's the underside of a 27.5m-high, four-block-long canopy designed by The Jerde Partnership, the LA-based firm behind public spaces in Roppongi Hills, Tokyo and, in the UK, masterplans for Coventry and Blackpool. It was built in 1995 – a bid for attention as the Strip merrily flung up mega-resorts and Downtown languished as its poor relation. The canopy has 12 million LEDs and hosts nightly sound and light shows. Cheesy? Of course. Also along East Fremont Street, check out the array of restored neon signs and the illuminated frontages of the city's oldest casinos, the 1951 Binion's (No 128) and the 1946 Golden Nugget (No 129). *425 E Fremont Street, T 678 5600, www.vegasexperience.com*

Welcome to Fabulous Las Vegas sign

Many cities have a welcome sign, but this is the only one we know of that features the word 'fabulous'. And it's not wrong. Commissioned in 1952 – the start of a boom decade for Las Vegas, as well as the new neon age – the sign needed to be special. Commercial artist Betty Willis completed it in 1959, creating a distinctive diamond shape and setting silver dollar coins behind each letter of Welcome, a reference to Nevada's Silver State moniker. The diamond is topped with a Googie starburst. Set on an island in the Strip, it wasn't the safest place to access and photo ops used to involve a game of chicken across the freeway. There is now a handy car park. The sign was never copyrighted, so you can buy the T-shirt or even, at Unica Home (see p086), the shower curtain. *Las Vegas Boulevard South/Russell Road*

HOTELS

WHERE TO STAY AND WHICH ROOMS TO BOOK

First-time visitors should stay in the thick of the action, on the Strip or not far off it. Las Vegas boasts more than half of the world's 20 largest hotels – the MGM Grand (see p030) has at least 5,000 rooms – so they can be pretty bland. Most of the hotels are within resorts, where the casino is king. The top choices are self-contained wings, which offer a more exclusive service – for example, Nobu (see p028) has just opened its first hotel, a 180-room boutique within Caesars Palace (see p080). The Cosmopolitan (opposite), launched in 2010, is a welcome experiment in independent cool.

The $8.5bn CityCenter development features the Aria hotel (see p024), a Mandarin Oriental (3752 Las Vegas Boulevard South, T 590 8888) and Daniel Libeskind's Crystals mall. Donald Trump arrived in 2008 and other big players have added towers – Encore (see p031) at Wynn, Palazzo at The Venetian (see p064), and Paradise and HRH at the Hard Rock (see p023). On a more lo-fi tip, two dying off-Strip hotels, Rumor (see p026) and Artisan (1501 W Sahara Avenue, T 1 800 554 4092), have been renovated into hip, non-gaming boutiques. But the economic havoc has turned this most extreme boom-and-bust town into a graveyard of doomed projects; the in-limbo Fontainebleau remains a major eyesore and legal wrangles over Norman Foster's seemingly finished Harmon could see it detonated without even opening.

For full addresses and room rates, see Resources.

The Cosmopolitan

Vegas' hippest resort arrived in 2010. The $3.9bn Cosmopolitan's coherent design, by a coterie of firms, mixes materials and textures – marble, granite, velvet, onyx and leather – with elan. There's much to praise here: a 20m chandelier (above) that envelops three floors of cocktailing; a dark, sexy lobby with a video installation; windows in the casino (previously unheard of); artists in residence; and an eschewing of ritzy tribute acts in favour of rooftop-pool gigs by the likes of Jay-Z and Brandon Flowers, and sessions by indie musos and DJs on the casino floor. Of the 2,995 chic rooms, more than 70 per cent have outside space (again, unusual for Vegas), including the Terrace One Bedroom (overleaf). The best overlook the iconic Bellagio fountain. *3708 Las Vegas Boulevard South, T 698 7000, www.cosmopolitanlasvegas.com*

Terrace One Bedroom, The Cosmopolitan

Palms

A short drive from the Strip, Palms is where Britney Spears embarked on her 55-hour marriage, perhaps after utilising the resort's multimillion-dollar recording studio, or maybe following one of the singles nights in Ghostbar (T 942 6832). There's wow-factor luxe here too. Themed Fantasy Suites have 'dancing' poles in the shower; the Hardwood Suite even has a basketball court (opposite). We prefer the Sky Villas and their cantilevered infinity jacuzzi pools, or, at ground level, the stylish Bungalows, whose decks overlook the steamy action by the pool (above). All 428 rooms were overhauled in 2012 by architects Klai Juba, using warm woods and velvet. Rejuvenate at the Drift Spa (see p088), which has Vegas' first hammam.
4321 W Flamingo Road, T 1 866 942 7777, www.palms.com

Bellagio

Now part of MGM Mirage, this was Steve Wynn's ultimate creation before he fell prey to the Wall Street sharks and had to start over, bouncing back with the Wynn (see p031). With 3,933 rooms, it's another mega-structure, but the vaguely Italian theme aims for sophistication and results in plenty of light, airy, classically inspired spaces. The shopping street, Via Bellagio, is upscale, both the Picasso and Le Cirque restaurants are excellent, and the Gallery of Fine Art is a bonus. And then there is the water feature: 34,000 sq m of lake with 1,200 'dancing' fountains, which you'll no doubt recognise from *Ocean's Eleven*. If you win big, party in the 380 sq m Chairman Suite (above), which has every kind of luxury and comfort, if rather bland decor.
3600 Las Vegas Boulevard South,
T 693 7111, www.bellagio.com

Hard Rock

This laidback hotel attracts a young, party-ready crowd, but the vibe is less plastic than at Palms (see p020). The Hard Rock theming isn't overwhelming and although it's off Strip (about a mile), you won't feel out of the action. Standard rooms are well equipped, comfortable and, by Las Vegas standards, positively cool, boasting Bose sound systems. Reserve the Pool Villa Suite Miami Vice (above) or, for your inner playboy, the Penthouse Real World Suite, which has a mirrored ceiling, a pool table and a bowling alley. The pool holds Rehab (read retox) parties on Sundays in summer: rock out with live bands and DJs or create a splash at the swim-up blackjack table. The Roman baths-style Reliquary Spa (see p089) provides welcome respite.
4455 Paradise Road, T 693 5000,
www.hardrockhotel.com

Aria

The focus here isn't on the party-all-night set, yet Aria avoids the pinky-raising that you might expect at, say, the Bellagio. The counterpoised curvilinear glass towers were designed by Pelli Clarke Pelli for MGM and opened in late 2009. Calling cards are the country's first Japanese Ganbanyoku stone beds at the 7,500 sq m metaquartzite spa, and a fantastic art collection that includes works by Tony Cragg, Antony Gormley and Maya Lin. The 4,004 mainly earth-toned rooms have window walls with views of Veer Towers (see p010); high-rollers should check into one of the Sky Suites, such as the One-Bedroom Penthouse (right). Highlights of the myriad nightlife options are the tapas and Spanish cuisine by chef Julian Serrano, Michael Mina's American Fish (see p054) and the gargantuan club Haze. *3730 Las Vegas Boulevard South, T 1 866 359 7111, www.arialasvegas.com*

Rumor

Like its sister property Artisan (see p016), known for its weekend after-hours parties and artist-themed rooms, Rumor is located away from the fray on Harmon Avenue. Its 150 rooms, designed by Tandem and Chemical Spaces, are arranged around a retro futuristic interior and a sprawling Palm Springs-style pool patio (opposite). Chinese foo dogs carved from Cantera stone sit in a lobby that feels like an ultra lounge, thanks to the vinyl seating and a Victoriana check-in desk; and Addiction Restaurant is as quirky, boasting chrome accents and transparent acrylic furniture. Book the sleek Premium Oasis Suite (above) for its elevated tub in the bedroom and easy access through patio doors to the cabana area. Rumor is a great option for those who want a fast-paced aesthetic with an easy-going Sunday attitude.
455 E Harmon Avenue, T 1 877 997 8667, www.rumorvegas.com

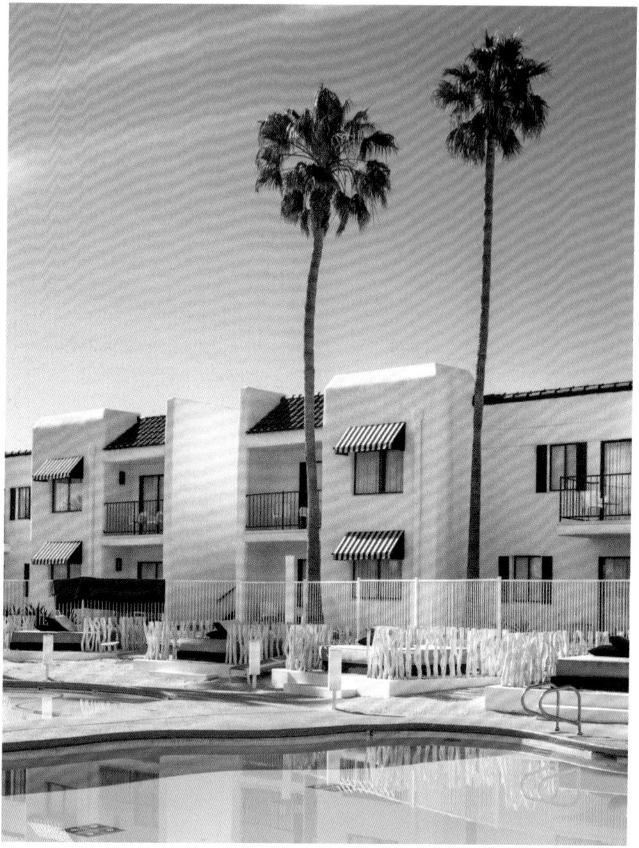

Nobu Hotel
The Rockwell Group's Nobu Hotel, the
first in the world, is a study in wood. The
lobby walls are a jigsaw of fir, oak and
hemlock blocks; basket-inspired abaca
booths define the restaurant; and rooms
such as the Luxury King (pictured) have
George Nakashima-style furniture in
teak and knotty pine. It's all rather Zen.
*Centurion Tower, Caesars Palace, 3570
Las Vegas Boulevard South, T 785 6677*

Skylofts

Designed as upscale metropolitan pieds-à-terre by Tony Chi, and secreted away on the 29th and 30th floors of the MGM, the 51 Skylofts are a revelation – minimalist white spaces with double-height lounges, 7.5m windows, mezzanine bedrooms and original pop art. Check-in is in your loft, with your butler, who will have drawn the infinity tub for your arrival. Freshen up in the rain immersion chamber and ponder the 15 pillow options. Your pad comes with a laptop, wi-fi, personalised stationery on request and more. The Skylofts range in size from a 130 sq m one-bedroom space (above) to 555 sq m with three bedrooms. For visitors with smaller budgets, The Signature at MGM Grand (T 1 877 612 2121) offers 'space-efficient' Petite King rooms. *3799 Las Vegas Boulevard South, T 1 877 646 5638, www.skyloftsmgmgrand.com*

Encore

When it opened in 2005, the $2.7bn Wynn (T 770 7000) was the most expensive hotel ever built. And it shows. Steve Wynn included a Ferrari dealership and a Manolo Blahnik store, both doing well, and there's a private golf course (see p092). In 2008, Wynn added the Encore tower to bring the total number of rooms close to 4,800. They are lavish but less chintzy (Encore Salon Suite, above) than many in the city, with floor-to-ceiling windows providing a great Strip view. The 550-plus Tower Suites make up the hotel-within-a-hotel and offer a separate check-in. Pitched at hedonists, the resort hosts a wild pool party, three upscale clubs (see p055) and no fewer than 10 fine-dining palaces, notably the Michelin-starred Chinese, Wing Lei.
3121 Las Vegas Boulevard South,
T 770 8000, www.wynnlasvegas.com

24 HOURS

SEE THE BEST OF THE CITY IN JUST ONE DAY

Vegas is a 24-hour town, so it's possible to cram a lot into one day. However, the Strip, essentially one giant nightspot, doesn't really wake up until late afternoon. Early risers (and the jet-lagged) can make the most of this and have a free-roaming morning without the crowds, and lovebirds can start as they mean to go on and get a licence and marry on the same day (see po34), although Nevada is not yet so liberal as to offer same-sex weddings. Meanwhile, the helicopter ride of your life, to the Grand Canyon, only takes a few hours – try Papillon (T 736 7243, www.papillon.com) – and it is arguably the greatest jackpot to be had on a Las Vegas trip.

The best breakfast is at the Wynn's (see po31) Buffet or poolside Tableau or, off-Strip, at Eat (opposite) and Chocolate & Spice (7293 W Sahara Avenue, T 527 7772), where Megan Romano's caramel brioches are legendary. A flutter is a must (see po36) at some point; tables operate 24/7. In the evening, choices are legion. You could try quiet drinks – a rarity – and artisan small plates at Italian wine lounge Onda (The Mirage, 3400 Las Vegas Boulevard South, T 1 866 339 4566), followed by acrobatics in Cirque du Soleil's *KÀ* at the MGM Grand (see po30). Like most shows in Vegas, this runs from Tuesday to Saturday. For dinner, try Twist (see po37). The wide-awake should then head to Artisan (see po16), Thursday through Sunday, for a dancefloor that doesn't really get going until 3am. *For full addresses, see Resources.*

11.00 Eat

The first stand-alone restaurant of former Strip chef Natalie Young, Eat is the place to come for a Southern US comfort-food brunch – artery-clogging dishes such as breaded fried steak and *huevos motuleños* (tortillas, eggs, black beans and cheese), as well as a range of delicious healthy salads. Architects CSP stripped back a dilapidated corner of an apartment block to its bare bones. The long redwood communal table was handcrafted by Zak Ostrowski, the bar was built from pallet wood, local artist Krystal Ramirez created the *I'll See You in the Flowers* mural and photography is by New Yorker Alice Gao. It's proved highly popular: be prepared to wait for a table at weekends. It's open from 8am until 3pm, and 2pm on Saturdays and Sundays. *707 Carson Street, T 534 1515, www.eatdtlv.com*

Graceland
WEDDING
CHAPEL
Presents A Storybook Chapel
619
Graceland
WEDDING
CHAPEL
JON BON JOVI

12.30 Graceland Wedding Chapel

If marriage is a gamble, then where better to wed than Vegas? For rock'n'roll nuptials, Graceland gets our vote. Brides can be given away by Elvis, who ends the ceremony with a rendition of 'Viva Las Vegas'. Pick up your licence from the Clark County Marriage Bureau at 201 Clark Avenue (T 671 0600).
619 Las Vegas Boulevard South,
T 382 0091, www.gracelandchapel.com

15.00 Bellagio

High-rollers and novices alike will want to gamble in the slickest environment in town. Nowhere will you totally escape bad carpets and the cacophonous clash of slot machines and muzak, but the ambience at the Bellagio and the Wynn (see p031) is more upmarket. Beginners can boost their confidence with free lessons at The Venetian (see p064), but dealers anywhere may be willing to teach you when it's quiet.

The game du jour is poker; blackjack and roulette are easier for first-timers to get the hang of. Be sure to fuel up before you embark on a session. There are numerous options in the resorts, of course, but if you are making your way here from Downtown in a taxi, take a detour via the excellent West Side robata grill Raku (T 367 3511). *3600 Las Vegas Boulevard South, T 693 7111, www.bellagio.com*

20.30 Twist

Celebrated French chef Pierre Gagnaire's first US restaurant is pure destination dining, nestled 23 storeys above the Strip in CityCenter, with similarly stratospheric prices. Adam D Tihany juxtaposed wood, glass and steel, and hung an industrial-looking wine cellar and 316 glass orbs from the ceiling. Sample the exemplary fusion cuisine in the seasonal Esprit tasting menu, which features dishes such as grilled Maine lobster with seaweed, and French pastry-inspired desserts. Twist opens for dinner only and closes on Sundays and Mondays. More dining options abound at Mandalay Bay, from Aureole (T 632 7401), also the work of Tihany, to Fleur (see p059), and Mix (T 632 7200), fronted by Alain Ducasse. *Mandarin Oriental, 3752 Las Vegas Boulevard South, T 1 888 881 9367, www.mandarinoriental.com/lasvegas*

22.30 Artifice

This casual neighbourhood lounge has exposed brick walls, rustic wood floors and comfy red-leather booths, and is decked out with work by local artists. Its theatre-like back room (pictured) acts as a stage for musicians, DJs and often the raunchy side-projects of Cirque du Soleil cast members. The witty cocktail menu names drinks after the regulars.
1025 S 1st Street, T 489 6339

URBAN LIFE
CAFÉS, RESTAURANTS, BARS AND NIGHTCLUBS

Las Vegas is known for the all-you-can-eat buffet, but recent years have seen an influx of restaurants that hold their own on the global culinary stage. The talent, menus and design are often imported from New York, San Francisco or Europe, so don't come looking for originality, but do expect big names, such as Thomas Keller, Alain Ducasse and Charlie Palmer. The excess of the buffets is now outdone by the gourmet tasting menus of chefs like Joël Robuchon at the MGM Grand (3799 Las Vegas Boulevard South, T 891 7433), Guy Savoy at Caesars (3570 Las Vegas Boulevard South, T 731 7286) and José Andrés at The Cosmopolitan (see p017), where he runs both the smart Jaleo and the whimsical China Poblano (see p048).

The re-emergence of a buzzy nightlife scene in old Vegas around East Fremont Street has been most welcome. Commonwealth (see p056), sister bar Park (No 506, T 834 3160) and Downtown Cocktail Room (111 Las Vegas Boulevard South, T 880 3696) serve modern takes on classic cocktails; also check out Velveteen Rabbit (1218 S Main Street, T 685 9645) and Artifice (see p038) in the Arts District.

In summer, don't miss the decadent daytime pool parties; we'd strip off at Marquee in The Cosmopolitan or at Encore Beach (see p031). The nightlife takes its cue from Ibiza and is built around superstar DJs. Plan ahead on weekends when the bachelor parties and LA crowd descend – peak hours are 1am to 4am.
For full addresses, see Resources.

Moon

On the top floor of Palms' Fantasy Tower, 150m up in the air, Moon is a 1,160 sq m club with panoramic Strip views through floor-to-ceiling windows and a huge, retractable roof for dancing under the twinkly stars. Designed by 9Group and 555 International, everything is gold and yellow, steel and glass, from a backlit hexagonal facade stretching from the bar up to the ceiling (above) to the tiled floor with traffic-activated lights (very *Saturday Night Fever*). Moon is a stalwart of the Palms (see p020) party scene, and in this fickle town, longevity is a sure sign that you must be doing something right. It opens at 10.30pm, Tuesdays, Fridays and Saturdays. Have a sharpener first on the cantilevered terrace of Ghostbar, one floor below. *4321 W Flamingo Road, T 942 6832, www.palms.com/nightlife/moon*

Social House
This Japanese/South-East Asian sushi and
sake lounge moved from Treasure Island
to set up in the swish Crystals mall (see
p062) and is all the better for it. A relaxed
take on the Orient, there's a moody vibe,
with dark woods, rich gold and bronze
lighting, antique newspapers, and design
elements informed by Asian icons such as
the bird's nest. Executive chef Jon Amorin
oversees some of the finest sushi on the
Strip – try the tempura lobster roll with
spicy tuna, cucumber, avocado, gobo and
sweet eel sauce – as well as fusion treats
such as Kobe sliders and tacos; dishes
are intended to be shared. The extensive
sake list is categorised by season and
best sampled in the $20-for-three flight.
Signature drinks include the Akita cocktail
(mandarin vodka, espresso, chocolate
and syrup) and teas, such as citrus oolong.
*Crystals, 3720 Las Vegas Boulevard South,
T 736 1122, www.socialhouselv.com*

Bouchon

Thomas Keller is one of America's hottest chefs, thanks to his three-Michelin-starred restaurants Per Se in New York and The French Laundry in California. To taste the maestro's cuisine (albeit cooked by Joshua Crain), head to this bistro for seasonal classics such as the *gigot d'agneau* (leg of lamb) and crème caramel. Given the dearth of breakfast spots in Vegas, thanks to the all-encompassing buffets, it's also a draw in the morning, especially the brunch at weekends (served until 2pm). Try the eggs any which way, French toast or sourdough waffles with bananas and maple syrup, accompanied by a bellini, of course. Take a seat either in Adam D Tihany's fancy interior – French pewter bar, mosaic floor, antique lighting – or outside by the pool. *The Venetian, 3355 Las Vegas Boulevard South, T 414 6200, www.bouchonbistro.com*

Fleur

Chef Hubert Keller has dived head-first into the small-plate concept at Fleur, with his mainly French-, Mediterranean- and American-inspired dishes. The restrained, modern rustic interior features mock stone walls, Currey & Company's forged-iron tree-branch chandeliers and an outer area set up like a patio with garden furniture. Drapes enclose private booths, although VIPs may prefer the first-floor wine loft, which seats four. Highlights on the menu include oysters on a bed of margarita sorbet, maple-glazed pork ribs and the headline-grabbing $5,000 burger (Wagyu beef, black truffles, foie gras and fries – with a bottle of 1995 Château Pétrus). We suggest you finish with the perfectly fluffy chocolate soufflé. *Mandalay Bay, 3950 Las Vegas Boulevard South, T 632 7200, www.mandalaybay.com*

Hakkasan
Not just a two-storey restaurant but also
three floors of nightlife, Hakkasan sprawls
over a vast 7,430 sq m. Carved marble and
latticed woodwork enclose intimate dining
spaces, as in London, although it's harder
to fathom the link between the delicate
Cantonese cuisine and the banging tunes.
But this is Vegas and no one really cares.
*MGM Grand, 3799 Las Vegas Boulevard
South, T 891 3838, www.hakkasanlv.com*

China Poblano

What's the point of being a famous chef if you don't get to goof around? José Andrés' buzzy eaterie is a celebration of Chinese and Mexican street food with an upscale slant. It's not fusion, yet there is cross-fertilisation in small plates such as taco of duck tongue and lychee (cleverly named *silencio*), and the cuisines complement each other surprisingly well. The menu is split into dim sum, noodles, soups and tacos, and includes ceviche and quesadilla. Seed Design's vivid decor features a ceiling covered in 100 bike wheels, Mexican tiles, restrooms papered with currency, and surrealist prints on the walls. We love the Cold Tea for Two – beer, green tea, lemon, tequila and Sichuan pepper served in a pot. *The Cosmopolitan, 3708 Las Vegas Boulevard South, T 698 7900, www.chinapoblano.com*

Hyde

Designed by Gulla Jonsdottir and Philippe Starck and secreted away in Bellagio, Hyde is styled on an opulent Tuscan villa. As you would expect, there's plenty of marble and leather, mahogany floors and chandeliers, but also more imaginative pieces such as Winnie Lui's 'Beads Octo' lights (above), Fabio Novembre's white polyurethane 'Nemo' chair, moulded to resemble a mask, and eclectic artwork. Showpiece cocktails include the liquid nitrogen Cable Car (rum, curaçao, orange juice), mixed table-side for maximum effect, and the Love Unit (vodka, grapefruit and red pepper juice), which may help on the intimate dancefloor. But the real draw is the unobstructed view of the hotel's legendary fountain show from a private perch on the terrace.
Bellagio, 3600 Las Vegas Boulevard South, T 693 8700, www.hydebellagio.com

Poppy Den

This Asian gastropub is an escape from the posh, chain-heavy Tivoli Village suburb in which it is located. Star chef Angelo Sosa's unique menu is a catch-all of Asian and US classics, but none the worse for that – try the crispy pork dumplings, miso salmon with shishito peppers or shrimp and grits. The main space has whitewashed rough plastered walls, dark hardwood flooring and exposed beams and girders; there's a separate red-and-black dining room with more of an oriental vibe if you so prefer. Park yourself at the polished granite bar for a sake or cocktail before dinner. Afterwards, retire upstairs for a post-prandial on the balcony or in the lounge (opposite), with its plush, buttoned seats, shagpile rug and birdcage chandelier. *Suite 180, 440 S Rampart Boulevard, T 802 2480, www.vegaspoppyden.com*

Tao

Asian-themed Tao, sister branch of the New York original, is the buzziest one-stop nightlife destination in Vegas. Inside the Tardis-like space, you'll find a lively bistro bar, a restaurant (above), two dance areas playing the usual hip hop and house, and a lounge. Popular items on the pan-Asian menu include the angry dragon roll and satay of Chilean sea bass – ordering an entrée gets you free entry (see what they did there?) to the club. To take in Tao's dimly lit, sexy atmosphere, rather than the hustle and bustle, dine early on a week night and leave Fridays and Saturdays to the bachelorette parties. The same team is behind the Italian-themed restaurant/club Lavo (T 791 1800) in the Palazzo. *The Venetian, 3355 Las Vegas Boulevard South, T 388 8338, www.taorestaurantlv.com*

American Fish

This restaurant provides a contemporary take on a traditional mountain lodge. Walls are panelled with sustainably harvested cherrywood and floors are fashioned out of timber dredged from the Great Lakes. On the ceiling, a Cor-ten steel sculpture is designed to evoke lily pads, and behind the elevated bar, a paper installation is inspired by the Minnesota Northwoods. The lower dining floor has a view of the show kitchen, from which we recommend chef Michael Mina's four-course tasting menu and wine pairing. However, the bar is an equally big draw here as its cocktail list is one of the most comprehensive on the Strip. Elsewhere in Aria, Jean Georges Steakhouse is a mecca for carnivores. Note that both restaurants shut at 10.30pm.
Aria, 3730 Las Vegas Boulevard South, T 877 230 2742, www.arialasvegas.com

Tryst

As you would expect from the Wynn (see p031), its flagship nightclub is a class act. According to Steve Wynn, Tryst, the $2.7m brainchild of club impresario Victor Drai and his team, paid for itself 10 times over in its first year. The space opens on to the hotel's waterfall and lagoon, which is illuminated at night, and has a patio offering loungers and chairs for posing and the scenic delivery of chat-up lines.

Inside, red-velvet walls and drapes, mirrored surfaces and red alligator-skin seating set the sexy tone. The music is wide-ranging, if safe. Further top clubbing options within the Wynn include the huge XS (T 770 7070), with its sophisticated vibe and an expansive pool patio, and Encore Beach, which becomes Surrender at night. *Wynn, 3131 Las Vegas Boulevard South, T 770 3375, www.trystlasvegas.com*

Commonwealth

On the corner of the Fremont East and 6th Street thoroughfare, the quirky two-floor Commonwealth is the best of the new crop of Downtown cocktail bars. The cavernous main room imitates the prohibition era, with its deep, leather booths beneath vaulted beamed ceilings, and dark wood mouldings over exposed brick, all dimly lit by chandeliers and candles. It hosts a roster of DJs and live bands. Above is a more intimate bar with a fascia covered in pennies, in addition to an expansive wraparound roof terrace. But the hippest part of Commonwealth is its bijou cocktail space, The Laundry Room, which seats about 20 and is hidden away behind a 'secret' door. It can only be reserved via an unlisted phone number (shoot the breeze with the bartender). *525 E Fremont Street, T 445 6400, www.commonwealthlv.com*

The Lady Silvia

Inspired by Prague's Strahov Monastery Library, this neo-gothic speakeasy sits in the heart of the Arts District. It's way too hip to provide any obvious signage – look for the silhouette of a bouncer on the tinted-glass doors. Inside the catacomb-esque hideout, it all feels a bit *Alice in Wonderland*. You'll discover black-and-white chequered floor tiles, a jade onyx bar counter, towering bookcases, vintage and Victorian-style furniture, electric candelabras and a grungy mixed-media mural by artist Steven Spann on the ceiling. The energy levels here are rather chameleonic – the chilled acoustic sets during early-evening happy hour on Fridays (5-8pm) crank up to thumping trance for a raucous weekend crowd. *900 Las Vegas Boulevard South, T 405 0816, www.theladysilvia.com*

Red Square

This bar/restaurant is as chilled as they come – and not just because of the sub-zero, walk-in Vodka Vault (they lend you a fur coat while you down a shot) and ice-topped bar that keeps your martini cool. Wander in past the decapitated Lenin statue (his head's in the freezer) to find an artfully conjured environment of faded Tsarist grandeur that blends red-velvet upholstery and chandeliers with communist posters. Try one of 200 kinds of vodka on offer or a cocktail such as the KGB (cucumber vodka, watermelon and chilli), and order caviar by the ounce. The food strays from Russian to French, Italian and American, via dishes such as beef short rib stroganoff with mushroom tagliatelle and truffle ricotta. Dinner only. *Mandalay Bay, 3950 Las Vegas Boulevard South, T 632 7407, www.mandalaybay.com*

1 Oak

Thanks to designers Munge Leung, this Vegas outpost of New York's upscale Chelsea club shares many traits, from the black-and-white herringbone entryway floor to the wagon-wheel chandeliers. Text from Darwin's *The Origin of Species* is etched in gold calligraphy in the hall leading to the main room, although lights are kept almost too low to see. It opens up to a sophisticated, 1,485 sq m space with caramel-coloured booths and original art by surrealist Roy Nachum on the walls. The centrepiece is a large DJ booth with state-of-the-art Avalon and Moonlighting sound and light systems by John Lyons. It's more relaxed but darker still in the back bar (above), where you'll be thankful for the LED-lit cocktail and drinks menu. *The Mirage, 3400 Las Vegas Boulevard South, T 588 5656, www.1oaklasvegas.com*

INSIDER'S GUIDE

SAMANTHA JO ALONSO, BOUTIQUE OWNER

Las Vegas born and bred, Samantha Jo Alonso is co-owner of the fashion boutique Fruition (4139 S Maryland Parkway, T 796 4139). She loves her city for the opportunities it offers: 'Vegas is all about play and exploration, and is full of people from all walks of life.'

On her days off, Alonso goes for breakfast at the Verandah in the Four Seasons (3960 Las Vegas Boulevard South, T 632 5121) before retail therapy at Monogram at The Cosmopolitan (see p017) or Crystals (3720 Las Vegas Boulevard South, T 590 9299); she also recommends Undefeated (see p082). She likes to have a leisurely lunch at the Thai restaurant Lotus of Siam (Suite A5, 953 E Sahara Avenue, T 735 3033), and afterwards makes a beeline to Luv-It Frozen Custard (505 E Oakey Boulevard, T 384 6452) or The Cupcakery (9680 S Eastern Avenue, T 207 2253) for a sweet treat.

In the evenings, after a flutter in The Cosmopolitan casino, she might eat at its STK Steakhouse (T 698 7990) and go clubbing at Marquee (T 333 9000). 'The hotel blends elegance with a youthful energy.' Alternatively, Commonwealth (see p056) is forging a 'new kind of Downtown', although she still loves the classic Peppermill Fireside Lounge (2985 Las Vegas Boulevard South, T 735 4177).

If she needs a break from the city, Alonso will escape to the bewitching scenery of nearby Red Rock Canyon (see p096) or to Willow Beach on the Colorado River, where she enjoys jet-skiing. *For full addresses, see Resources.*

ARCHITOUR

A GUIDE TO THE CITY'S ICONIC BUILDINGS

Fantasy architecture and disorientating replicas may dominate Las Vegas, but that's not all there is. Nor are they unimpressive. Veldon Simpson took inspiration as much from John Portman as ancient Egypt to create the pyramid at Luxor (see p074). And who wouldn't want to ride a travelator over Stubbins Associates' Rialto Bridge at The Venetian (3355 Las Vegas Boulevard South, T 414 1000)?

Movie-sets are on the slide, however. The latest architectural trends are a Manhattanification, notably with the measured glass towers at CityCenter (see p010) and The Cosmopolitan (see p017), and a glamorisation of the Downtown area around Symphony Park. Here, the warped-steel Center for Brain Health (see p066) landed in 2010, followed two years later by The Smith Center (see p068), an art deco-style home for the Vegas Phil and Nevada Ballet, as well as new premises for City Hall (495 Main Street) – a seven-storey collection of eco-friendly glass boxes by local firm JMA.

The city's incessant reinvention does mean that old gems are often trampled in the rush to build the new. There to pick up the pieces is Neon Museum (see p077). Enter through the former lobby of the 1961 La Concha Motel to witness Googie history, such as the 1965 sign from the imploded Stardust casino (its Electra-Jag lettering was replaced by Helvetica in 1991). To see intact motel signage, drive from East Fremont Street towards Boulder Highway. *For full addresses, see Resources.*

Las Vegas Academy

Reno architects George A Ferris & Son's statuesque exemplar of Mayan art deco went up in 1930 and was the only high school in town for two decades. Thankfully, it survived the midcentury modern mania that swept through the city, and still stands proud in Downtown, with its bright-red paint job and original stuccoed friezes of crouching Indians, twisting vines, bunches of grapes and zodiacal motifs. Since 1993, it has been the home of the Academy of International Studies, Performing and Visual Arts, with an interior updated to withstand the inevitable histrionics of a group of dance and drama students. The artwork by graduating years (1941 to 1988) that adorned the forecourt has now been blasted clean but their memory lives on in replica plaques set in a new welcome wall.
315 S 7th Street

Lou Ruvo Center for Brain Health
Frank Gehry's building for the Keep
Memory Alive foundation is felicitously
unforgettable. We've seen his crumpled
facades before, but here the shell gets
equal billing from within, framing an
airy space illuminated by 199 windows.
Medical facilities are housed in a more
conventional structure behind; the pair
symbolising the two halves of the brain.
888 W Bonneville Avenue, T 263 9797

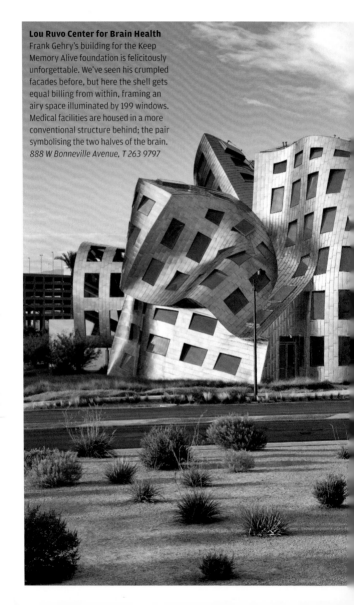

The Smith Center

Vegas finally got a cultural venue of note in 2012. Constructed using 2,458 tonnes of Indiana limestone, it was designed by architects David M Schwarz in an art deco style inspired by the Hoover Dam (see p098), although the 17-storey belltower lends it an ecclesiastical feel. The opulent lobby (opposite) boasts Fior di Pesco marble flooring, cylindrical chandeliers, aluminium latticework and Benjamin Victor's *Genius in Flight* sculpture. The acoustically engineered 2,050-seat Reynolds Hall is now the home of the city philharmonic and also hosts Broadway and dance shows that used to skip Vegas. An outdoor stage is framed by Tim Bavington's *Pipe Dream* sculpture based on Aaron Copland's *Fanfare for the Common Man*. *361 Symphony Park Avenue, T 749 2000, www.thesmithcenter.com*

Emergency Arts

This 1940s midcentury modern box, with its cantilevered canopy and strip windows, was once the Fremont Medical Center. The derelict building has been resurrected as Emergency Arts (an apt name considering the closure of many of Vegas' headline galleries) by Jennifer and Michael Cornthwaite of the Downtown Cocktail Room (see p040). Examination rooms and nurses' stations have been turned into gallery and event spaces rented by artists, fashion designers, musicians et al; the place buzzes on the first Friday of the month when it's open house. At other times, drop by The Beat Coffeehouse (T 385 2328) for poetry readings and gigs, and to buy vinyl. In the bathrooms, it still feels as if you're there to give a urine sample.
520 E Fremont Street, T 300 6268, www.emergencyartslv.com

Clark County Government Center
In any other city, this expressionistic structure might seem a little adventurous for a local government administration centre. But this is Las Vegas, where the inclusion of a pyramid raises few eyebrows. The 1995 building, in steel and concrete, is clad in red sandstone, evoking the colours of the surrounding desert. Looking partly like a Wild West fortress, partly like a colosseum, it is laid out in a semicircle around an amphitheatre, as if opening its arms in welcome. The Center is the work of architects Fentress Bradburn with the Domingo Cambeiro Corporation, and its multistorey rotunda has a dramatic interior with stucco-finished balconies and desert-flower-inspired sculptural lamps. The pyramid café opens weekdays till 2.30pm.
500 S Grand Central Parkway,
www.clarkcountynv.gov

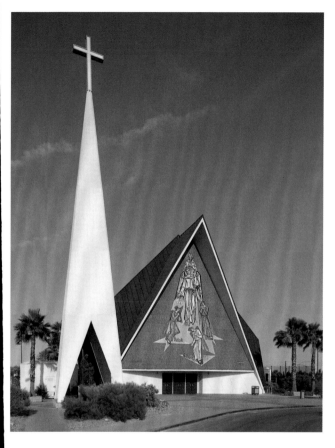

Guardian Angel Cathedral

Should you be seeking salvation after a gambling frenzy or from a surfeit of Sin City PoMo, head to this little beauty. Its architect, the late Los Angeles-based Paul Revere Williams (see p077), was the first African-American member, then fellow, of the American Institute of Architects, and designed homes for the stars, including Frank Sinatra and Lucille Ball. Run by Viatorian clerics, the cathedral seats 1,100 and its Sunday masses are always heavily attended by tourists. As well as the fabulous fresco above the entrance, there's a swirling mural behind the altar, and the stained-glass windows in the building's triangular 'ribs' include one by Isabel Piczek that depicts casinos. Another Vegas touch is the gift shop at the back. *302 Cathedral Way, T 735 5241, www.lasvegas-diocese.org*

Luxor
Designed in 1993 by Veldon Simpson, the
Luxor's 107m-tall black-glass pyramid
forms the world's largest atrium, served
by elevators that travel at 39 degrees.
By night a 'Sky Beam' shoots straight up
into space and can be seen from 400km
away. But it also attracts a huge pillar of
insects, and the bats that feed on them,
creating its very own ecosystem.
3900 Las Vegas Boulevard South

Huntridge Theater

Designed as a cinema in 1944 by S Charles Lee, this streamline moderne building, which has a 23m tower topped by 305m of neon tubing, has been empty since 2004 and should consider itself lucky to be still standing. Few structures are allowed to sit and crumble, however elegantly, for so long in Vegas. As Downtown redevelops apace, its site is crying out to the condo brigade. Although the Huntridge is on the National Register of Historic Places and is supposedly 'safe' until at least 2017, its owner has already tried to overturn the order banning its demolition. Over time, it has functioned as a makeshift venue for Sunday mass and, in its later years, hosted concerts. A campaign was launched in 2013 to restore the building and turn it into a community arts venue.
1208 E Charleston Boulevard

Neon Museum

In a dusty yard behind a wire fence resides decades' worth of signage (overleaf), an invaluable typographical and visual history of Vegas. Here lies a rusting, two-storey letter 'W' from the 1950s Showboat Hotel; there lies the 4.6m silver slipper from the eponymous casino, which Howard Hughes bought up in 1968 because the lights of the revolving shoe disturbed him in his Desert Inn room over the street. This is the storage site of the non-profit Neon Museum, which saves and restores signs. In 2006, the curators acquired the iconic concrete parabolic arches of Paul Revere Williams' La Concha Motel lobby to serve as the visitor centre (above). Book in advance for a guided morning or evening tour. Staff are full of stories of old Vegas.
770 Las Vegas Boulevard North, T 387 6366, www.neonmuseum.org

SHOPPING

THE BEST RETAIL THERAPY AND WHAT TO BUY

When you're not gambling, eating or drinking, chances are you'll be shopping. The high-end resorts all have upscale retail areas ready to either help you celebrate a win or compound your losses with a consolation purchase. The Wynn (see p031) is the only hotel in the world to contain a Ferrari dealership. It also houses Oscar de la Renta, Dior Homme, Brioni and Manolo Blahnik. Bellagio (see p022) has similarly classy labels, including Prada, Tiffany & Co and Gucci. For a hoot, hit the promenades beneath the fake blue skies at The Venetian (see p064) or, our favourite, The Forum Shops at Caesars Palace (3570 Las Vegas Boulevard South, T 731 7110), which has some 160 stores where you can splash the cash, from Fendi to Valentino, amid fountains, statuary and restaurants.

Unique local shops are harder to find. Off-Strip, try Undefeated (see p082), Unica Home (see p086) or concept space Urban Ranch General Store (Suite 105, 6985 W Sahara Avenue, T 368 2601). For classic kitsch, drop by The Funk House (1228 S Casino Center Boulevard, T 678 6278) and Retro Vegas (1131 S Main Street, T 384 2700). If your dates coincide, go gallery-hopping in the Arts District on the first Friday of the month (www.firstfridaylasvegas.com), when the doors are thrown open all evening. Creative hubs with more regular programming include Emergency Arts (see p070) and The Arts Factory (107 E Charleston Boulevard, T 383 3133). *For full addresses, see Resources.*

Brett Wesley Gallery

Designed by owner Brett Sperry, this gallery's exterior honours midcentury modern architecture by way of a rising concrete canopy over an expansive glass front. Inside, it's full-on contemporary, all stained hardwood floors, exposed beams and a glass staircase. As in Artifice (see p038), Sperry's bar across the street, paintings and sculptures by local artists are on show here, alongside international work by the likes of John Bell, Julian Opie and Marilyn Minter, all available to buy. The exhibitions lean towards evocative pieces, such as the exploratory oil paintings in Kristine McCallister's 'Coming of Age' (above). One of the first purpose-built galleries to open downtown, it's a pioneer for Vegas' burgeoning artistic community. *1112 S Casino Center Boulevard, T 433 4433, www.brettwesleygallery.com*

Undefeated
In a city where leather slip-ons for the
casino floor are the default footwear,
this slimline, monochrome, collectable-
sneaker gallery is a godsend. Simply
decorated with a blown-up photo of
Aussie mixed martial artist Ian Schaffa
(ironically, not undefeated) and the
shop logo, it also sells caps and tees.
*Suite 400, 4480 Paradise Road,
T 732 0019, www.undefeated.com*

Skins 6|2 Cosmetics

The first US outpost of the family-owned
Dutch company Skins 6|2 was designed
by Amsterdam firm UXUS and is located
within The Cosmopolitan (see p017).
The emporium features a concrete floor,
white-oak and Formica furniture, Jean
Pelle's 'Bubble' chandeliers and a ceiling
of embossed tin tiles repeated on the
double front doors. Elsewhere in the vast
store, an entire wall is filled with mirrors
of all shapes and sizes hanging beneath
a clutch of CB2 'Eden' pendant lamps. But
the real draw is the high-end, 60-brand
cosmetic menu that includes products
from Creed, Atelier Cologne, Maison
Francis Kurkdjian and Santa Maria Novella,
most of which are unique to the market.
*The Cosmopolitan, 3708 Las Vegas
Boulevard South, T 698 7625,
www.cosmopolitanlasvegas.com*

John Varvatos

It was a no-brainer really, John Varvatos in the Hard Rock, and this fashion store for hard-livin' dudes draws a similar crowd to the hotel's main music venue, The Joint. Taking inspiration from Varvatos' flagship shop in the former CBGB in New York's The Bowery, there's plenty of masculine metal and wood, an urban-cowboy-esque seating area with faux-hide furnishings, a Playboy-Mansion-style chandelier and a 9m video wall showing classic rock promos. Although the setting is a little ham-fisted, and the store is incongruously situated between a tattoo parlour and a Pink Taco, that doesn't detract from the offerings, which include all three Varvatos lines – Collection, Star USA and Converse – and the only James Trussart guitars within state limits.
Hard Rock, 4455 Paradise Road,
T 693 6370, www.hardrockhotel.com

Unica Home
Despite downsizing from this warehouse, Unica Home still carries a fine selection of items by designers from Alessi to Zanuso and vintage pieces by the likes of Ettore Sottsass, Alvar Aalto and the Eameses. Or go online to pick up cheesy gifts such as a Welcome to Fabulous Las Vegas shower curtain ($29) by Izola. *Suite C, 4065 W Mesa Vista Avenue, T 616 9280, www.unicahome.com*

SPORTS AND SPAS
WORK OUT, CHILL OUT OR JUST WATCH

The point of sports in Las Vegas is generally not to take part but to bet on them. The city is flooded with visitors during key US events because gambling is illegal in some states, whereas Nevada welcomes it. Sportsbooks (betting shops) in every casino provide walls of TV screens and booths so you can watch matches from all over the globe. For expert gamblers, the World Series of Poker is held every year at the Rio All-Suite hotel (3700 W Flamingo Road, T 777 7650); winners can pocket nearly $9m (see p036 for gambling lessons). Live sport includes boxing (see p094) and rodeo, both of which take place at the Thomas & Mack Center (4505 S Maryland Parkway, T 895 3761). It also hosts everything from basketball to the Monster Jam extreme-truck-racing championships.

Visitors who want more exercise than dice-throwing will find that all the resorts have pools and gyms, as well as first-class spas; we recommend Drift in Palms Place (4321 W Flamingo Road, T 944 3219) for its beautiful mosaicked hammam. At Mandalay Bay (see p009), you can even scuba dive with sharks – and remember this is the middle of the desert. Those down on their luck may prefer to let off steam at The Gun Store (2900 E Tropicana Avenue, T 454 1110), where you can take out your frustration by firing an AK-47. Out of town, go rock climbing and desert driving in a Humvee at Red Rock Canyon (see p096) or boating on Lake Mead.
For full addresses, see Resources.

Reliquary Spa & Salon

As you might expect, the city of excess is also serious about relaxation. With roughly 50 spas in the major resorts alone, you can hardly throw a hot stone without hitting a hammam. The best and most popular are often Turkish- or Roman-style, such as Sahra (T 698 7171) at The Cosmopolitan and this 2,320 sq m spa at The Hard Rock. Reliquary features mosaic patterns in polished concrete tile and white Venetian plaster finishes, with private cabana-style alcoves off the main pool, as well as a salon and fitness centre. Specialised treatments include a Russian deep-tissue massage and the signature ancient cane ritual, here called 'Drum Sticks', of course, in which bamboo reeds are used to 'beat, tap and roll' the body to rebalance the chakras.
*Hard Rock, 4455 Paradise Road,
T 693 5520, www.hardrockhotel.com*

Las Vegas Motor Speedway

The Stardust Hotel opened the first motor-racing track in Vegas in 1966 to attract thrill-chasing high-rollers, and it also hosted the Can-Am championship. However, it closed in 1970 and speed freaks had to wait almost three decades for a replacement – the 142,000-capacity retro-styled Las Vegas Motor Speedway, devised by Talladega Superspeedway designer William W Moss. The four tracks host irregular events on Sundays, but the best time to visit is in early March to see the highly entertaining NASCAR Sprint Cup. If you prefer to be behind the wheel, schools like Exotics Racing (T 405 7223) offer the opportunity to drive a Ferrari, Lamborghini, Aston Martin or Porsche round the circuit (from $200 for five laps). *7000 Las Vegas Boulevard North, T 1 800 644 4444, www.lvms.com*

Wynn Golf Course

Proof that anything is possible in Vegas comes in the form of Wynn's golf course in the desert – all 18 holes of it, perfectly manicured to rather disarming shades of green. Construction involved moving roughly 600,000 cubic metres of earth to sculpt the various elevated sections, the planting of 100,000 shrubs and the relocation of 1,200 trees. It was designed by Steve Wynn and Tom Fazio, the course architect who remodelled Augusta, and finishes with a flourish at the 18th with a waterfall and the Stratosphere Tower (see p012) in the distance. Golfers might also want to tee off at the nearby Las Vegas Country Club (T 734 1132) or head half an hour out of town to the lovely Cascata (T 294 2005), set among the red rock hills.
*3131 Las Vegas Boulevard South,
T 770 4653, www.wynnlasvegas.com*

Bathhouse

There is no shortage of good spas in Vegas; every resort has its own. But their design remains largely conventional (see p089), apart from at THEhotel's Bathhouse, where a minimal setting lifts the experience. The work of New York designer Richardson Sadeki (who was behind NYC's Bliss Spas), the Bathhouse's slate walls and floors, 'rainfall corridors' and use of glass create a soothing Zen ambience where the only thing that's fluffy is the towels. Begin with a signature soak (women only; choose from aromapothecary, Ayurvedic or black moor mud) in a huge, softly lit tub beneath a 7m ceiling (above), or a spell in the eucalyptus steam room. Among the treatments are a pure oxygen facial, a 50-minute gents' facial and a crème brûlée mani-pedi.
THEhotel at Mandalay Bay, 3950 Las Vegas Boulevard South, T 1 877 632 7300

Johnny Tocco's Boxing Gym

If Vegas were a sporting hero, it'd be a boxer: it has the posturing, the bravado, the money and the grit. The Thomas & Mack Center (see p088) hosts big fights, as do many casinos. For a workout of your own, head to Johnny Tocco's. If that sounds too hard-core, at least go to admire the exterior murals (pictured).
9 W Charleston Boulevard, T 367 8269, www.jtboxing.com

ESCAPES

WHERE TO GO IF YOU WANT TO LEAVE TOWN

Once you've lived in Vegas' brilliant, brassy bubble for a day or two, chances are you'll be itching to get away from the neon. The city is surrounded by dramatic desert scenery. Helicopter rides to the West Rim of the Grand Canyon take less than half a day (see p032), or a full day to the more impressive South Rim with Scenic Airlines (T 638 3300, www.scenic.com). Take to the road to explore Death Valley and end up in Tahoe, taking in ghost town Bodie – a once thriving gold-mining burg – along the way. There are two spectacular Mojave Desert day trips closer to town: Valley of Fire State Park (opposite) and Red Rock Canyon. The latter, 27km from the Strip, offers rock climbing, riding and walking, and a scenic drive. You can do it in a day, but better to stay at the slick Red Rock Casino Resort & Spa (11011 W Charleston Boulevard, T 797 7777).

If watery pursuits appeal, Lake Mead is a 180km-long reservoir less than an hour from town; base yourself at the Mediterranean-inspired Hilton Lake Las Vegas (1610 Lake Las Vegas Parkway, T 567 4700). For winter sports, head to Mount Charleston, a 45-minute drive, and overnight in a log cabin at the Lodge (5375 Kyle Canyon Road, T 872 5408). More extreme types should head two-and-a-half hours north-east to Zion National Park (www.nps.gov/zion) in Utah to rappel down sandstone cliffs, hike through slot canyons and take an all-terrain vehicle through Coral Pink Sand Dunes. *For full addresses, see Resources.*

Valley of Fire State Park

Flame-red sandstone rocks, licked into other-worldly contortions (and, more surprisingly, shapes including a poodle and an elephant) by 150 million years of wind and water erosion give this 182 sq km state park its name. It's a compelling taste of the Mojave Desert wilderness, 89km north-east of Las Vegas, which can be enjoyed from the air-con sanctuary of a hire car (loaded with chilled drinks and snacks – even the ubiquitous restaurant mogul Wolfgang Puck hasn't ventured out here). For the perfect day trip, head to the Hoover Dam (overleaf) early in the morning to beat the crowds, rent a boat on Lake Mead for a floating lunch, then drive along the scenic Northshore Road to the Valley of Fire in time to enjoy the late-afternoon light on the rocks.
T 397 2088, www.parks.nv.gov/vf.htm

Hoover Dam

Concrete fans can get their fix at the
Hoover Dam, the 6.7-million-tonne stopper
to the Colorado River near Boulder City,
48km from Vegas. During construction it
took two years just to pour the concrete.
On eventual completion in 1935, the dam
was the tallest in the world at 221m and
contained more masonry than the Great
Pyramid of Giza. Its engineering feats
were matched by a modernist aesthetic
and the odd deco flourish. LA architect
Gordon Kaufmann simplified the original
designs, reducing ornamentation and
blending the towers along the dam's crest
into the main structure. Bas-reliefs by
artist Oskar Hansen adorn the central
towers, which house the lift shafts that
take visitors 160m down to the power
plant. If you don't have time to drive here
and take a tour, fly over by helicopter
en route to the Grand Canyon (see p102).
T 494 2517, www.usbr.gov/lc/hooverdam

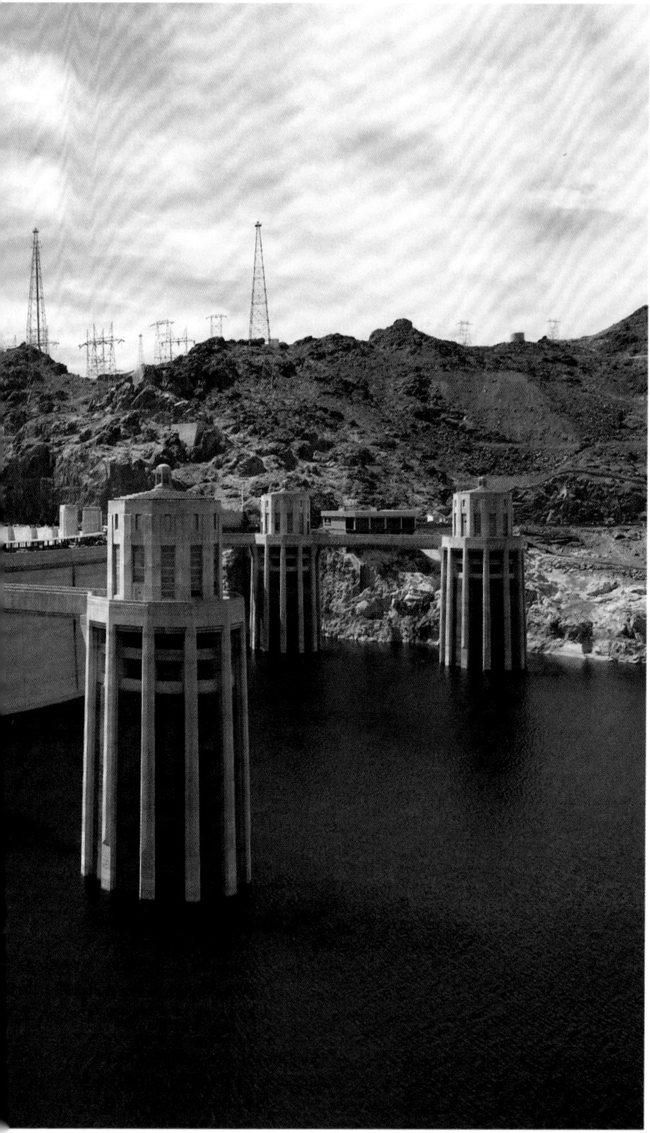

Amangiri, Utah

The approach to Amangiri, along a winding road flanked by the mountains of Utah's Canyon Country, sets the scene for an awe-inspiring stay. About a four-hour drive from Vegas, the resort's design – natural materials, outward focus, monumental scale – is informed by the raw, sparse beauty that surrounds it. The expansive Amangiri Suite includes a sky terrace, a desert lounge (above) and pools. The 2,322 sq m spa has walnut-lined treatment rooms and takes inspiration from Navajo healing traditions. Alternatively, a massage by the step pool (opposite) comes with sublime views. Explore the property's 243 hectares on foot or horseback; scenic flights transport you to Lake Powell, Monument Valley and Bryce Canyon.
1 Kayenta Road, Canyon Point,
T 435 675 3999, www.amanresorts.com

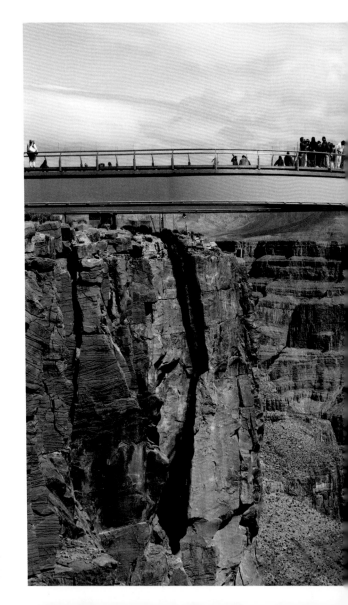

Grand Canyon Skywalk
At Grand Canyon West, the nearest and narrower end of the canyon, 193km from Las Vegas, you can step 21m into thin air. Well, actually you'll be supported by MRJ Architects' 600-tonne glass-and-steel structure, owned by the native Hualapai tribe, although vertigo sufferers may not enjoy registering the 1,200m void between them and the canyon floor. *www.grandcanyonwest.com*

NOTES
SKETCHES AND MEMOS

1

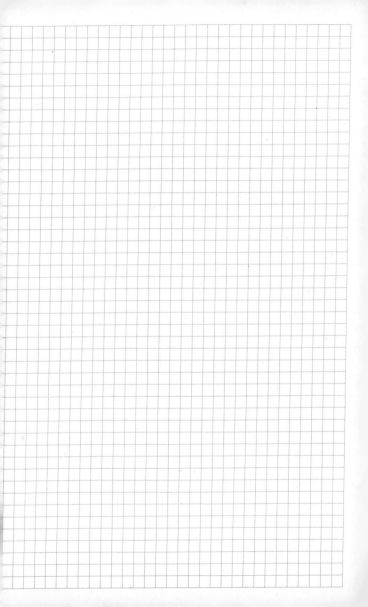

RESOURCES
CITY GUIDE DIRECTORY

A
American Fish 054
Aria
3730 Las Vegas Boulevard South
T 877 230 2742
www.arialasvegas.com
Artifice 038
1025 S 1st Street
T 489 6339
www.artificebar.com
The Arts Factory 080
107 E Charleston Boulevard
T 383 3133
www.theartsfactory.com
Aureole 037
Mandalay Bay
3950 Las Vegas Boulevard South
T 632 7401
www.aureolelv.com

B
Bathhouse 093
THEhotel at Mandalay Bay
3950 Las Vegas Boulevard South
T 1 877 632 7300
www.mandalaybay.com
The Beat Coffeehouse 070
Emergency Arts
520 E Fremont Street
T 385 2328
www.emergencyartslv.com
Bellagio 036
3600 Las Vegas Boulevard South
T 693 7111
www.bellagio.com
Binion's 014
128 E Fremont Street
T 382 1600
www.binions.com

Bouchon 044
The Venetian
3355 Las Vegas Boulevard South
T 414 6200
www.bouchonbistro.com
Brett Wesley Gallery 081
1112 S Casino Center Boulevard
T 433 4433
www.brettwesleygallery.com

C
Caesars Palace 080
3570 Las Vegas Boulevard South
T 731 7110
www.caesarspalace.com
Cascata 092
1 Cascata Drive
T 294 2005
www.cascatagolf.com
China Poblano 048
The Cosmopolitan
3708 Las Vegas Boulevard South
T 698 7900
www.chinapoblano.com
Chocolate & Spice 032
7293 W Sahara Avenue
T 527 7772
www.chocolatenspice.com
City Hall 064
495 Main Street
www.lasvegasnevada.gov
Clark County Government Center 072
500 S Grand Central Parkway
www.clarkcountynv.gov

HOTELS
ADDRESSES AND ROOM RATES

Amangiri 100
Room rates:
double, from $1,100;
Amangiri Suite, $3,600
1 Kayenta Road
Canyon Point
Utah
T 435 675 3999
www.amanresorts.com

Aria 024
Room rates:
double, from $100;
Sky Suite, $500;
One-Bedroom Penthouse Suite, $650
3730 Las Vegas Boulevard South
T 1 866 359 7111
www.arialasvegas.com

Artisan 016
Room rates:
double, from $40
1501 W Sahara Avenue
T 1 800 554 4092
www.artisanhotel.com

Bellagio 022
Room rates:
double, from $160;
Chairman Suite, from $6,000
3600 Las Vegas Boulevard South
T 693 7111
www.bellagio.com

The Cosmopolitan 017
Room rates:
double, from $245;
Terrace One Bedroom, $400
3708 Las Vegas Boulevard South
T 698 7000
www.cosmopolitanlasvegas.com

Encore 031
Room rates:
double, from $190;
Tower Suite, from $540;
Encore Salon Suite, $1,100
Wynn
3121 Las Vegas Boulevard South
T 770 8000
www.wynnlasvegas.com

Hard Rock 023
Room rates:
double, from $50;
Pool Villa Suite (Miami Vice), $675;
Penthouse Real World Suite, $7,000
4455 Paradise Road
T 693 5000
www.hardrockhotel.com

Hilton Lake Las Vegas
Resort & Spa 096
Room rates:
double, from $140
1610 Lake Las Vegas Parkway
Henderson
T 567 4700
www3.hilton.com

Mandalay Bay 009
Room rates:
double, from $130
3950 Las Vegas Boulevard South
T 632 7777
www.mandalaybay.com

Mandarin Oriental 016
Room rates:
double, from $245
3752 Las Vegas Boulevard South
T 590 8888
www.mandarinoriental.com/lasvegas

MGM Grand 030
  Room rates:
  double, $115
  3799 Las Vegas Boulevard South
  T 891 1111
  www.mgmgrand.com
Mount Charleston Lodge 096
  Room rates:
  cabin, from $190
  5375 Kyle Canyon Road
  Mount Charleston
  T 872 5408
  www.mtcharlestonlodge.com
Nobu Hotel 028
  Room rates:
  double from $200;
  Luxury King, $230
  Centurion Tower
  Caesars Palace
  3570 Las Vegas Boulevard South
  T 785 6677
  www.nobucaesarspalace.com
Palms 020
  Room rates:
  double, from $100;
  Fantasy Suite, from $100;
  Bungalow, $3,000;
  Sky Villa, from $10,000;
  Hardwood Suite, $25,000
  4321 W Flamingo Road
  T 1 866 942 7777
  www.palms.com
Red Rock Casino Resort & Spa 096
  Room rates:
  double, from $170
  11011 W Charleston Boulevard
  T 797 7777
  www.redrock.sclv.com

Rumor 026
  Room rates:
  double, from $70;
  Premium Oasis Suite, $115
  455 E Harmon Avenue
  T 1 877 997 8667
  www.rumorvegas.com
The Signature at MGM Grand 030
  Room rates:
  Petite King, $280
  MGM Grand
  145 E Harmon Avenue
  T 1 877 612 2121
  www.signaturemgmgrand.com
Skylofts 030
  Room rates:
  One-bedroom Skyloft, from $750;
  Three-bedroom Skyloft, $5,000
  MGM Grand
  3799 Las Vegas Boulevard South
  T 1 877 646 5638
  www.skyloftsmgmgrand.com
Wynn 031
  Room rates:
  double, from $200
  3131 Las Vegas Boulevard South
  T 770 7000
  www.wynnlasvegas.com

WALLPAPER* CITY GUIDES

Executive Editor
Rachael Moloney

Editor
Jeremy Case
Authors
Bridget Downing
Max Plenke

Art Director
Loran Stosskopf
Art Editor
Eriko Shimazaki
Designer
Mayumi Hashimoto
Map Illustrator
Russell Bell

Photography Editor
Elisa Merlo
Assistant Photography Editor
Nabil Butt

Chief Sub-Editor
Nick Mee
Sub-Editor
Farah Shafiq

Editorial Assistant
Emma Harrison

Interns
Karen Lohana
Mai Nguyen

Wallpaper* Group Editor-in-Chief
Tony Chambers
Publishing Director
Gord Ray
Managing Editor
Oliver Adamson

Wallpaper* ® is a registered trademark of IPC Media Limited

First published 2007
Revised and updated 2012 and 2013

All prices are correct at the time of going to press, but are subject to change.

Printed in China

PHAIDON

Phaidon Press Limited
Regent's Wharf
All Saints Street
London N1 9PA

Phaidon Press Inc
180 Varick Street
New York, NY 10014

Phaidon® is a registered trademark of Phaidon Press Limited

www.phaidon.com

A CIP Catalogue record for this book is available from the British Library.

© 2007, 2012 and 2013
IPC Media Limited

ISBN 978 0 7148 6644 4

PHOTOGRAPHERS

Adrian Gaut
Grand Canyon
Skywalk, pp102-103

Misha Gravenor
Bouchon, p044

Erik Kabik
Hard Rock, p023
Reliquary Spa &
Salon, p089

Darius Kuzmickas
Las Vegas city view,
inside front cover
Veer Towers, p010
Eiffel Tower, Paris Las
Vegas, p011
Stratosphere Tower,
pp012-013
Fremont Street
Experience, p014
Welcome to Fabulous
Las Vegas sign, p015
The Cosmopolitan,
p017, pp018-019
Bellagio, p022
Aria, pp024-025
Rumor, p026, p027
Nobu, pp028-029
Eat, p033

Graceland Wedding
Chapel, pp034-035
Bellagio, p036
Twist, p037
Artifice, pp038-039
Moon, p041
Social House, pp042-043
Fleur, p045
Hakkasan, pp046-047
China Poblano, p048
Hyde, p049
Poppy Den, p050, p051
American Fish, p054
Commonwealth,
pp056-057
The Lady Silvia, p058
Red Square, p059
1 Oak, pp060-061
Samantha Jo Alonso, p063
Las Vegas Academy, p065
Lou Ruvo Center for
Brain Health, pp066-067
The Smith Center,
p068, p069
Emergency Arts,
pp070-071
Clark County Government
Center, p072
Guardian Angel
Cathedral, p073
Luxor, pp074-075
Huntridge Theater, p076
Neon Museum, p077

Brett Wesley Gallery, p081
Undefeated, pp082-083
Skins 6|2 Cosmetics, p084
John Varvatos, p085
Unica Home, pp086-087
Las Vegas Motor
Speedway, pp090-091
Johnny Tocco's
Boxing Gym, pp094-095
Valley of Fire State
Park, p097
Hoover Dam, pp098-099

LAS VEGAS
A COLOUR-CODED GUIDE TO THE HOT 'HOODS

SOUTH STRIP
Marvel at the huge luxury hotels, boasting great views of Las Vegas' fantasy skyline

NORTH STRIP
The economic climate has turned it into a wasteland but Messrs Wynn and Trump survive

DOWNTOWN
Come for the retro Fremont Street lights and casinos, and stay for the emerging bar scene

CENTRE STRIP
The heart of the nightlife district is lined with miniature European cities, naturally

ARTS DISTRICT
A proliferation of galleries has transformed this still edgy area into a creative hub

PARADISE
Ordinary Vegas is typified here by low-rise sprawl but the Hard Rock keeps it unreal

For a full description of each neighbourhood, see the Introduction.
Featured venues are colour-coded, according to the district in which they are located.